ILLINOIS

BY COLLEEN SEXTON

BELLWETHER MEDIA • MINNEAPOLIS, MN

Blastoff! Discovery launches a new mission: reading to learn. Filled with facts and features, each book offers you an exciting new world to explore!

BLASTOFF! UNIVERSE

BLASTOFF! Beginners — GRADE K

BLASTOFF! READERS — GRADES 1-3

DISCOVERY — GRADE 4

This edition first published in 2022 by Bellwether Media, Inc.

No part of this publication may be reproduced in whole or in part without written permission of the publisher.
For information regarding permission, write to Bellwether Media, Inc., Attention: Permissions Department,
6012 Blue Circle Drive, Minnetonka, MN 55343.

Library of Congress Cataloging-in-Publication Data

Names: Sexton, Colleen A., 1967- author.
Title: Illinois / by Colleen Sexton.
Description: Minneapolis, MN : Bellwether Media, Inc., 2022. | Series: Blastoff! Discovery: State Profiles | Includes bibliographical references and index. | Audience: Ages 7-13 | Audience: Grades 4-6 | Summary: "Engaging images accompany information about Illinois. The combination of high-interest subject matter and narrative text is intended for students in grades 3 through 8"– Provided by publisher.
Identifiers: LCCN 2021019675 (print) | LCCN 2021019676 (ebook) | ISBN 9781644873847 (library binding) | ISBN 9781648341618 (ebook)
Subjects: LCSH: Illinois–Juvenile literature.
Classification: LCC F541.3 .S48 2022 (print) | LCC F541.3 (ebook) | DDC 977.3–dc23
LC record available at https://lccn.loc.gov/2021019675
LC ebook record available at https://lccn.loc.gov/2021019676

Editor: Kate Moening   Designer: Andrea Schneider

Printed in the United States of America, North Mankato, MN.

TABLE OF CONTENTS

FROZEN FALLS

In winter, the waterfalls in Starved Rock State Park freeze. Experienced ice climbers scale the falls. They climb from the canyon floors to the tops of the bluffs!

A school bus winds between tall trees. Students have arrived at Starved Rock State Park for a field trip! They start down a trail lined with oak trees and wildflowers. Their guide describes how **glaciers** made 18 **canyons** that cut through the park's sandstone **bluffs**.

STARVED ROCK
STATE PARK

ABRAHAM LINCOLN PRESIDENTIAL
LIBRARY AND MUSEUM

CAHOKIA MOUNDS STATE
HISTORIC SITE

MILLENNIUM PARK

NAVY PIER

Atop a bluff, the students see the Illinois River below. They spot white pelicans on the water. Then they watch a **barge** move through a lock and dam on the river. Finally, the group heads into a canyon. Tall waterfalls pour over cliffs onto the canyon floor. Welcome to Illinois!

Illinois is in the **Midwest** region of the United States. This tall, narrow state covers 57,914 square miles (149,997 square kilometers). Wisconsin borders Illinois to the north. Iowa and Missouri lie across the Mississippi River to the west. The Ohio River forms the southern border with Kentucky. Illinois shares its eastern edge with Indiana. Northeastern Illinois stretches along the shore of Lake Michigan.

Chicago sits on Lake Michigan. It is the largest city in Illinois. The capital city, Springfield, lies in the center of the state.

WISCONSIN

ROCKFORD

AURORA

LAKE
MICHIGAN

CHICAGO

NAPERVILLE

MISSISSIPPI
RIVER

JOLIET

PEORIA

ILLINOIS

SPRINGFIELD

INDIANA

THE LAND
OF LINCOLN

Illinois is known
as the Land of
Lincoln. Abraham
Lincoln lived in the
capital, Springfield.
He was elected
president in 1860.

OHIO RIVER

KENTUCKY

7

ILLINOIS'S BEGINNINGS

CAHOKIA MOUNDS
STATE HISTORIC SITE

People first arrived in Illinois about 12,000 years ago. They hunted animals and gathered plants for food. Over time, Native Americans formed many tribes, including the Fox, Sauk, and Kickapoo. These groups built villages, planted crops, and traded goods.

A LOST CITY

About 1,000 years ago, Native Americans built the city of Cahokia in southern Illinois. They constructed temples and homes on earthen mounds. Around 20,000 people may have lived in Cahokia. The city was abandoned by 1400. No one is sure why.

In 1673, the French began to explore Illinois. Fur traders and **missionaries** established a **settlement**. More Europeans soon followed. They built farms and towns in southern Illinois. The population grew steadily after Illinois became the 21st state in 1818. The U.S. government made **treaties** with Native Americans. These treaties pushed all Native Americans westward, out of Illinois.

NATIVE PEOPLES OF ILLINOIS

Illinois is named for the Illinois tribes that lived there for centuries. The Fox, Sauk, and Kickapoo were the most recent native residents. Illinois has no government-recognized tribes today.

FOX

- Original lands in northern and western Illinois from the mid-1700s to the 1830s
- Descendants largely in Iowa, Kansas, and Oklahoma
- Also called Meskwaki

SAUK

- Original lands in northwestern Illinois from the mid-1700s to the 1830s
- Descendants largely in Iowa and Oklahoma
- Also called Sac

KICKAPOO

- Original lands in north-central Illinois
- Descendants largely in Texas and Mexico

Most of Illinois is a flat **plain**. It was once covered by **prairie** grasses. Today, its rich soil makes Illinois an important farming state. The land slopes upward to rolling hills and valleys in the northwest. To the south, the Shawnee Hills feature river bluffs and wooded hills. Lowlands stretch along the Mississippi River at the state's southern tip.

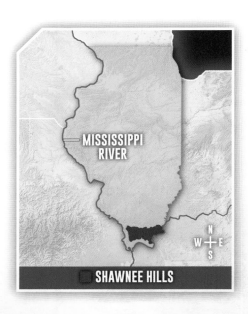

MISSISSIPPI RIVER

N
W E
S

SHAWNEE HILLS

SHAWNEE HILLS

ILLINOIS'S FUTURE: CLIMATE CHANGE

Scientists predict that a warmer climate will bring changes to Illinois. There may be more droughts in summer. Floods may increase in other seasons.

SPRING
HIGH: 60°F (16°C)
LOW: 39°F (4°C)

SUMMER
HIGH: 83°F (28°C)
LOW: 62°F (17°C)

FALL
HIGH: 63°F (17°C)
LOW: 42°F (6°C)

WINTER
HIGH: 34°F (1°C)
LOW: 18°F (-8°C)

°F = degrees Fahrenheit
°C = degrees Celsius

Illinois has cold winters and hot summers. The south is warmer and wetter than the north. Weather can change quickly when winds sweep across the prairie. Tornadoes are possible in spring and summer. Blizzards can strike in winter.

11

NORTHERN RACCOON

Illinois's forests and fields shelter many animals. White-tailed deer nibble on leaves. Raccoons and minks hunt mice and bullfrogs. Monarch and buckeye butterflies sip nectar from goldenrod and yellow coneflowers. Cardinals, blue jays, and goldfinches flit around backyard birdfeeders all year.

MONARCH BUTTERFLIES

Beavers build dams on Illinois's lakes and streams. In marshes, muskrats make lodges from cattails and other plants. Walleye and northern pike hunt young largemouth bass in rivers and lakes. Marshes and river valleys protect **migrating** birds. Ducks and geese fly through the region in spring and fall.

AMERICAN GOLDFINCH

AMERICAN BEAVER

MALLARD DUCK

12

WHITE-TAILED DEER

Life Span: up to 3 years
Status: least concern

white-tailed deer range =

LEAST CONCERN	NEAR THREATENED	VULNERABLE	ENDANGERED	CRITICALLY ENDANGERED	EXTINCT IN THE WILD	EXTINCT

PEOPLE AND COMMUNITIES

In the late 1800s, Illinois's rich farmland and busy cities drew many **immigrants**. They came from European countries such as Germany, Ireland, Sweden, and Austria. Today most Illinoisans have **ancestors** from Europe. Many Black or African Americans and Hispanic Americans live in the state. Smaller groups of Asian Americans and Native Americans call Illinois home. Many recent newcomers hail from Mexico, India, and Poland.

ILLINOIS'S FUTURE: A DECREASING POPULATION

Illinois's population is decreasing. People are leaving for other states. Because of this, the state could get less money from the government. It may also lose out on new businesses coming to the state.

CHICAGO

FAMOUS ILLINOISAN

Name: Michelle Obama

Born: January 17, 1964

Hometown: Chicago, Illinois

Famous For: First Lady of the United States from 2009 to 2017 who advocated for health and education, author of the best-selling memoir, *Becoming*, and host of *The Michelle Obama Podcast* and the children's television show *Waffles + Mochi*

Illinois has a population of about 12.8 million people. Most live in the state's northern cities. Two out of every three residents call the Chicago area home. Central and southern Illinois are mostly **rural**. People live on farms and in small towns.

WILLIS TOWER

SKY HIGH

The Great Chicago Fire of 1871 destroyed much of the city. The people who helped rebuild Chicago developed the world's first skyscrapers.

Chicago began as a French settlement in the 1770s. It grew into a world-famous city known for its industry and **diversity**. Today, Chicago is the country's third-largest city and a trade center. Its Willis Tower is the country's second-tallest skyscraper. It offers an amazing view of Chicago! Parks and beaches stretch along Lake Michigan. The lakefront includes Millennium Park's fountains, gardens, and sculptures. Navy Pier features an amusement park.

Chicago is known for the arts. The city boasts several major theater companies. The Chicago Symphony Orchestra is respected around the world. The Art Institute of Chicago features an important collection of **impressionist** paintings.

THE ART INSTITUTE OF CHICAGO

NAVY PIER

INDUSTRY

O'HARE INTERNATIONAL AIRPORT CHICAGO

More than 370 destinations worldwide.

UNITED

Illinois is a transportation center. Trucking and shipping companies use the state's airports, waterways, and network of highways. Chicago is also the busiest city in the country for railroads. Illinois's rich soil has been its most important **natural resource** for centuries. Today, the state's farmers are leading growers of corn and soybeans. They also raise hogs, cattle, and turkeys.

A RIVER ROUTE

The Illinois Waterway allows cargo to be shipped from Lake Michigan to the Mississippi River. Canals dug between rivers and lakes created this route.

Factory workers produce farming equipment such as harvesters and plows. These machines are shipped around the world. Workers also make chemicals, machinery, and rubber products. Most Illinoisans have **service jobs**. They work in finance, **insurance**, and the government. **Tourism** supports service workers with jobs in hotels and restaurants.

SERVICE WORKER

INVENTED IN ILLINOIS

CELL PHONE
Date Invented: 1973
Inventors: Martin Cooper, Motorola

FERRIS WHEEL
Date Invented: 1893
Inventor: George Ferris

DISHWASHER
Date Invented: 1886
Inventor: Josephine Cochrane

ZIPPER
Date Invented: 1893
Inventor: Whitcomb L. Judson

CHICAGO HOT DOG

Illinoisans treasure their classic foods. The Chicago hot dog is topped with mustard, sweet relish, onions, and tomatoes. A dill pickle, peppers, and celery salt are the finishing touches. Deep-dish pizza and Italian beef sandwiches are other popular meals. The horseshoe sandwich comes from Springfield. This open-faced sandwich features ham or beef topped with french fries and cheese sauce.

POP!

Popcorn is the official snack food of Illinois. Chicagoans mix cheese popcorn and caramel popcorn to make a sweet and salty treat!

Neighborhood restaurants offer flavors from many different countries. Pierogi are a popular Polish dish. These dumplings feature a variety of fillings. Illinoisans explore more dishes at the Taste of Chicago. This summer food festival offers samples from many restaurants.

TASTE OF CHICAGO

HORSESHOE SANDWICH

4 SERVINGS

Have an adult help you make this Springfield specialty!

INGREDIENTS

1 9-ounce bag frozen french fries

1 pound ground beef

4 slices bread, toasted

CHEESE SAUCE

Use a premade sauce. Make it special with seasonings such as salt, pepper, hot sauce, or Worcestershire sauce.

DIRECTIONS

1. Preheat the oven to 400 degrees Fahrenheit (204 degrees Celsius). Bake the french fries on a baking sheet for 20 minutes or until golden brown.

2. Divide the ground beef into four equal parts and form into patties.

3. Fry the patties in a large skillet over medium-high heat until well done, about 4 minutes per side.

4. Place a slice of toasted bread on each of four dinner plates. Top each slice with a hamburger patty. Place cooked french fries on top of each patty.

5. Pour cheese sauce on top. Serve immediately.

WRIGLEY FIELD
HOME OF
CHICAGO CUBS

| RANGERS | 1 | FINAL |
| CUBS | 3 | |

TOYOTA

Sports fans in Illinois have a lot to cheer about. Chicago's professional teams play baseball, football, basketball, hockey, and soccer. The Chicago Bandits fastpitch softball team also draws crowds.

CHICAGO BULLS

Illinoisans enjoy the outdoors. In summer, they hike and camp in state parks. Lakes and rivers are popular for swimming, boating, and fishing. In winter, residents go sledding, cross-country skiing, and ice skating. Chicago draws people to its theaters, museums, and concert halls. Illinoisans learn about the **Civil War** at the Abraham Lincoln Presidential Library and Museum in Springfield. The cities of Belleville and Elgin host audiences for their fine symphony orchestras.

NOTABLE SPORTS TEAM

Chicago Bandits
Sport: National Pro Fastpitch softball
Started: 2005
Place of Play: Parkway Bank Sports Complex

Illinoisans begin the year at the Illinois Snow Sculpting Contest in Rockford. Carving teams from around the state craft snowy masterpieces. Summer festivals feature bands playing jazz, blues, and Latin music, among others. In June, Superman fans show off their costumes at the Superman Celebration in Metropolis. Port Byron offers the Great River Tug Fest every August. Teams from Illinois and Iowa play tug-of-war across the Mississippi River.

Springfield hosts the Illinois State Fair every August. Crowds enjoy farm exhibits, carnival rides, and concerts. At the Village of Cultures, fairgoers sample foods from around the world. The fair helps Illinoisans celebrate their state!

ILLINOIS STATE FAIR

GOING GREEN

Chicago celebrates St. Patrick's Day every year by dyeing the Chicago River green!

CHICAGO RIVER

1832

Sauk warrior Black Hawk leads three tribes in the Black Hawk War, but the U.S. government wins the war and pushes the tribes out of Illinois

ABOUT 1050

Native people flock to the city of Cahokia, causing a population explosion

1763

France gives up Illinois to Great Britain after the French and Indian War

1818

Illinois becomes the 21st state

1673

French explorers Louis Jolliet and Jacques Marquette are the first Europeans to visit the region

1871

The Great Chicago Fire destroys nearly all of downtown Chicago

2016

The Chicago Cubs win the World Series for the first time since 1908

2008

Illinois senator Barack Obama is elected the 44th president of the United States

1860

Springfield lawyer Abraham Lincoln is elected the 16th president of the United States

Nicknames: The Prairie State, The Land of Lincoln

Motto: State Sovereignty, National Union

Date of Statehood: December 3, 1818
(the 21st state)

Capital City: Springfield ★

Other Major Cities: Chicago, Aurora, Rockford, Joliet, Naperville, Peoria

Area: 57,914 square miles (149,997 square kilometers);
Illinois is the 25th largest state.

Population

12,812,508
(2020)

STATE FLAG

ILLINOIS

Illinois's state flag was adopted in 1915. It has a white background with the state seal in the center. A bald eagle holds a shield with stars and stripes. They stand for the original 13 states. A banner in the eagle's beak features the state motto, "State Sovereignty, National Union." A rock shows the date of statehood and the date the state seal was adopted. The sun rising over a prairie represents Illinois's future. The state name was added to the bottom of the flag in 1970.

INDUSTRY

Main Exports

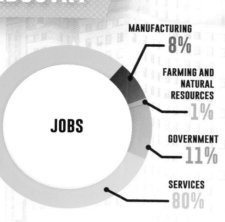

JOBS

MANUFACTURING
8%

FARMING AND NATURAL RESOURCES
1%

GOVERNMENT
11%

SERVICES
80%

chemicals

corn

transportation equipment

processed foods and beverages

Natural Resources
coal, limestone, petroleum, sand, gravel, soil

GOVERNMENT

19 ELECTORAL VOTES

Federal Government
17 REPRESENTATIVES | **2** SENATORS

IL

USA

State Government
118 REPRESENTATIVES | **59** SENATORS

STATE SYMBOLS

STATE BIRD
NORTHERN CARDINAL

STATE FISH
BLUEGILL

STATE FLOWER
VIOLET

STATE TREE
WHITE OAK

GLOSSARY

ancestors—relatives who lived long ago

barge—a long, flat-bottomed boat used to transport cargo on rivers and lakes

bluffs—cliffs or steep banks that often overlook a body of water

canyons—deep valleys that have steep sides

Civil War—a war between the Northern (Union) and Southern (Confederate) states that lasted from 1861 to 1865

diversity—having a variety of people or things from many different backgrounds

glaciers—massive sheets of ice that cover large areas of land

immigrants—people who move to a new country

impressionist—a style of painting that uses dabs of paint to give the effect of light in a scene

insurance—a business in which people pay money for protection against injuries or damages

Midwest—a region of 12 states in the north-central United States

migrating—traveling from one place to another, often with the seasons

missionaries—people sent to a place to spread a religious faith

natural resource—a material in the earth that is taken out and used to make products or fuel

plain—a large area of flat land

prairie—related to a large, open area of grassland

rural—related to the countryside

service jobs—jobs that perform tasks for people or businesses

settlement—a place where newly arrived people live

tourism—the business of people traveling to visit other places

treaties—official agreements between two groups

AT THE LIBRARY

Gregory, Josh. *Illinois*. New York, N.Y.: Children's Press, 2018.

Kelley, K.C. *Chicago Cubs*. Mankato, Minn.: Child's World, 2019.

Micklos Jr., John. *Illinois*. New York, N.Y.: Cavendish Square Press, 2020.

ON THE WEB

FACTSURFER

Factsurfer.com gives you a safe, fun way to find more information.

1. Go to www.factsurfer.com.

2. Enter "Illinois" into the search box and click 🔍.

3. Select your book cover to see a list of related content.

INDEX